Opted Out
of the *Real Job*

Opted Out of the *Real Job*

Build Your Small and Smart ONLINE TEACHING BUSINESS

By Elena Mutonono and Veronika Palovska

Copyright © 2017 by Elena Mutonono and Veronika Palovska

All rights reserved. This book or any portion thereof may not be reproduced or used in any manner whatsoever without the express written permission of the authors except for the use of brief quotations with attribution to the authors.

Requests to the authors for permission should be addressed to the contacts listed here: **optedoutlife.com/contact**.

Disclaimer: The advice and strategies contained herein may not be suitable for your situation. The authors shall not be liable for any loss of profit or any other commercial damages, including but not limited to special, incidental, consequential, or other damages.

Cover and interior design by Veronika Palovska

Editing by Dave Nelson, thegrammargeek.com

ISBN-13: 978-1978149441
ISBN-10: 1978149441

Dedication

We dedicate this book to all the brave teachers and coaches who have found the courage to opt out into the unknown world of entrepreneurship.

To you, who refuse to tolerate the status quo, who opt out of security to work smarter, who invest their heart today with the hope of a better tomorrow, who treasure being small and memorable over huge and faceless, who design remarkable and creative programs and choose to make meaning in the world that chases money - you are braving the deep blue sea to impact this world with your message.

This world will never be the same because of the decision you've made. We want you to know that you are not alone. Together we can make our small efforts count.

Contents

Introduction 9

1 Reboot Your Mindset 11

2 Discover Your Niche 21

3 Make a Mark on Social Media 29

4 Build a Blog That Matters 39

5 Craft a Website That Works for You 47

6 Develop an Outstanding Personal Brand 55

7 Detect Your Ideal Client 63

8 Hack Your Pricing 73

9 Get Your First Clients Online 81

10 Find Money to Invest in Yourself 89

11 Create an Online Course 99

12 Delegate to Work Smarter 109

Conclusion 119

Acknowledgements... 123

About the authors.. 127

Further Resources 129

Endnotes.. 131

Introduction

This handbook will help you get started with your small and smart online business. Often, people look for quick tips and easy solutions, ignoring the foundation on which everything will be built.

In this book, we focus on the foundation, the core of your business. We dig deeper and answer questions that people might overlook while distracted by the rush toward "shiny objects." We encourage you to take your time going through this book so you can process the concepts more deeply.

We wrote this book to encourage those who don't think they can escape the rat race. We challenge you to "opt out" when you feel as though your current environment is stifling and is impeding your growth.

We are Elena Mutonono and Veronika Palovska—two English teachers who opted out to work online. You will find some generic classroom and teaching references in this book—nothing too complicated.

We believe in the freedom and flexibility that an opted-out life brings. We've experienced the benefits of growing, creating, and living on our own terms thanks to the beautiful concept of opting out.

We believe in working smarter, which means focusing on what matters and outsourcing or automating the rest. We build small businesses, not six-figure empires. We believe in the driving force of creativity that molds us into the people we were destined to be.

To get even more out of this book, get the Opted Out Journal at **optedoutlife.com/journal** and work through the reflective questions chapter by chapter.

Chapter 1
Reboot Your Mindset to Think Like a Business Owner

Imagine installing new software on a twenty-year-old computer. You spend time toiling and sweating to make it work. You take the beast apart, hoping to rewire the ancient machine. You wonder why the new software still isn't functioning and spend months learning from YouTube enthusiasts how an old computer can be revived.

You may make some progress, and your success will fool you into thinking you've got it all together. Then you discover there are more problems than you had anticipated. You feel overwhelmed, overworked, and frustrated. You forget why you wanted to install the software on this computer in the first place.

When you opt out of your *real job* and step into the world of online entrepreneurship, you will experience the struggle of installing the new software on an ancient machine. You're now running a business, and knowing the tools and techniques isn't enough.

You need a "new computer."

In the very beginning, your mindset is the old computer that you'll try hard to rewire and reboot. Fortunately, renewing your mindset is easier than buying a new computer, but you need to understand why it's necessary and how to do it.

Why you need a new mindset

Entrepreneurship is a new lifestyle that is unlike any other profession. In teaching, for instance, you have a predictable set of goals that you need to accomplish in your classroom. If you're not careful, stepping into the shoes of an entrepreneur will make you feel like you need to replicate familiar steps by just copying them in a new format.

But that rarely works, because as an entrepreneur, you engage in a high-risk game with rules you may not recognize. Until you accept it, you'll be in a predicament of forcing the old computer to work with the new software.

In a recent survey in our Opted Out Facebook community (facebook.com/groups/optedout), the overwhelming majority of participants (mostly teachers) shared that if they had a business question, they would choose to **find**

the answer on their own. No one considered hiring a coach a helpful alternative. Conversations with successful teachers-turned-entrepreneurs revealed the same results: a high reluctance to trust a coach and a tendency to figure things out on their own.

Yet in a different survey, when asked the best way to learn a language, many chose **hiring a teacher** as the most effective option. Studying on their own would take place when they couldn't find a language teacher to help.

Why is that? The main reason is, in the unfamiliar format of running a business, teachers **aren't aware of what they don't know,** so they're more inclined to try things on their own, not realizing how much time this is going to take. Meanwhile, in the familiar language-learning environment, they understand how the process is going to move along faster with fewer glitches if people **find an experienced teacher**.

Clearly, these teachers-turned-entrepreneurs need new mindsets.

How to change your mindset

Now that we know that mindset change is one of the basics to run a successful small business, let's see how exactly you can adopt the mindset of an entrepreneur.

#1: Visualize your business.

Teachers know how to visualize their lesson plans, how to set goals and objectives to achieve specific and measurable outcomes at the end of a 45-minute slot. Yet we find it difficult to see what we want our business to achieve in one year.

Take the time daily to *visualize* your business.

Think about the impact it will make on the people who come in contact with it. Think about your brand promise. Think about what this business will help *you* achieve in your personal and professional life.

Don't just swap one workplace for the other. Don't just move your regular job online. Rather, redesign your thinking to fit your big dream.

#2: Get comfortable with fear, failure, imperfection, and other unpleasant distractions.

According to BusinessDictionary, an entrepreneur is someone who is "highly optimistic (otherwise nothing would be undertaken)."

Successful entrepreneurs look at failure as a predictable outcome of trying something new. They aren't afraid to get a "bad grade," for they see it as a part of learning.

Professionals in *real jobs* struggle with failure

and fear (among other things) because they are *professionally striving for perfection.*

Are you willing to let the fear and failure go in order to make progress with your online business? Try reframing these and other unpleasant concepts (like setting deadlines, for instance) as welcome sojourners in your life who make no decision about your future.

- Failure: the evidence of trying something new.

- Fear: the sign of a bigger vision for your business.

- Deadlines: the constraints that help you progress over time.

#3: Find help.

Hiring a coach will yield the best results. Because it is a financial decision, you will have to do some planning and be prepared to act after every session. But hiring someone who has been where you're planning to walk is both inspiring and energizing.

On top of that, **you don't know what you don't know**, and having someone by your side who has walked this road will give you clarity and a sense of direction. It will cut out the unnecessary wandering that happens when you try and figure out things on your own.

Besides, it's a bit hypocritical (especially when you offer services) to ask people to pay *you* when you aren't willing to invest in yourself.

Your mindset change is a daily exercise in which you flex your entrepreneurial muscles until your body is toned to withstand the stressors of the entrepreneurial world. Use a journal to track your progress, and make the above three mind-setting routines your life if you want to succeed.

Each chapter in this book will take you one step deeper into the Opted Out life, where you abandon the *real job* mindset and craft a small and smart business of your own. Please use your Journal exercises to help these principles sink in and mold your new life.

Chapter 2
Discover Your Niche

When you first venture into the online business world, you have to add new expressions to your vocabulary and wrap your head around concepts that don't make much sense to you. One of them seems to be particularly popular and confusing: a niche.

Every online marketing guru talks about it, it's being discussed in communities, and you can't stumble on a blog post or a podcast episode where the dreaded word isn't mentioned at least once.

So, what is a niche, anyway? In marketing, a niche is a small, specific, and well-defined segment of a market. Once you find your niche, you focus all your marketing efforts only on this small group of people. And because marketing is nothing but offering solutions, we may say that having a niche means solving a specific problem of specific people.

Interestingly, even after reading countless materials, taking classes, and discussing the matter on forums, many online teachers and coaches still find themselves in the dark about the niche-finding process. Moreover, many of them resist the idea of niching down.

After talking to a number of teachers and coaches at different stages of the niche-finding process, and after reflecting back on when we struggled with this issue ourselves, we identified the issue. Teachers and coaches think that limiting themselves to a specific group of people runs counter to the essence of what they want to do: help as many people as they can.

Being of service is the reason you became a teacher or a coach in the first place, right? And now someone tries to convince you that you have to say no to people who need your help, just for the sake of "marketing."

You may understand and acknowledge that, from a marketing point of view (whatever that means), niching is important. But you still don't want to do it because it's against your nature. You can't help it. And you are not alone.

We're here to guide you through it.

Why helping everyone isn't helping everyone

Before we get practical about finding your niche, let's talk about why niching down is not an obstacle in the way of helping people, but quite the opposite.

1. It makes you visible.

When you know who the people you're talking

to are, it's not so hard to figure out where they hang out online and mingle with them so you can listen to them — and talk to them.

Once you get to know your dream clients, you'll never again struggle to come up with content ideas. And because you'll talk about the things that are most relevant to them and you'll appear in places where they like to spend their time, the chances that you'll bump into each other are high.

2. It makes you relevant.

Both your free content and your paid products and services should solve problems. That's your job. And the effectiveness of your solutions depends on how clearly defined the problem is.

In other words, if the problem you're trying to solve is too generic or not defined at all, you can't help anyone because you're just scratching the surface. Conversely, when you zero in on a specific problem, you can dig deeper and make an impact.

3. It saves your sanity and brings your clients better results.

Having a niche makes everything easier — not just marketing but also teaching or coaching itself. When you develop materials (such as tutorials, lesson plans, or workbooks) for a specific group of people who experience a specific problem, you can test it, get feedback, fine-tune it, and then use it with an unlimited number of clients, again and again.

You become an expert in solving that particular problem. When someone asks you for help, you offer them a tried and tested solution, without having to come up with a new solution that may or may not work.

4. It enables you to go beyond one-on-one sessions.

When you know your dream clients and their problem, you can package yourself more creatively than "one hour for $20, five hours for $90 — save $10!" You can develop packages and products that bring you freedom and that bring your clients results.

You can stop selling your time and start selling solutions.

5. It helps you brand yourself.

Last but not least, your niche is an important part of your brand. It's what makes you stand out in the ocean of language teachers or fitness coaches and position yourself as an expert.

In summary, helping everyone is not helping everyone. Being a jack-of-all-trades makes it hard for people who need you to find you online. Furthermore, your time, energy, and experience are spread so thin that you don't give your clients enough of anything.

Conversely, focusing on a particular problem puts you in a position where you can solve the problem—and that's how you opt out of the **illusion** of helping people and move into the **reality** of helping people.

Which one do you prefer?

How to (really) find your niche

Now that it's clear that niching down isn't a mysterious marketing trick but something that helps you help people, you may wonder how to make it happen. Where do you even start?

The question isn't easy to answer, because there is no universal, step-by-step process. One thing is clear, though. The worst way to start is by thinking about which niche is the most profitable one.

The thing is, your small and smart online business doesn't need a large number of followers to thrive and make an impact. What it needs is for you to stop caring about numbers (how many people are interested in the topic and how much they're willing to pay) and instead put your energy into finding people with the same worldview who genuinely care about your message. You need to find your tribe.

In the journal, you'll find exercises to help you gain clarity and translate your insights into a niche.

An important thing to note here is that niche-finding is a never-ending process. As you start working with real clients, your niche will evolve and change.

Of course, it won't change dramatically. Your *why* — the only thing that never changes — will be your anchor. With a strong core message, you'll be able to weather all the storms and stay true to your vision, while giving yourself enough space to move, breathe, and explore.

Chapter 3
Make a Mark on Social Media

The social media world is a magical place. Even when starting from scratch, with no connections and no budget, you can find your tribe and make a mark.

Let's talk about how to get the most out of the social media wonderland and how to engage, educate, entertain, and market to your people without turning them off and burning yourself out.

Choose the right platforms

To make the most out of social media, don't spread yourself too thin. You don't have to be everywhere. Focus on the platforms where your dream clients are. Having a niche makes the task easier, because when you know who your dream clients are, it's easy to find them online.

If you're just getting started, choose *one* channel. Learn all about the platform's culture, build your following, and (partly) automate your presence. Don't add more platforms until you master this one. It's better to be a rockstar on one social media platform than to struggle with five of them.

Social media culture

Creating a profile and getting started on a new

social media platform feels like entering a foreign country: you don't understand the language, you don't know where to go, and even the easiest task makes you sweat. Moreover, your lack of understanding of local culture may be perceived as rudeness—no matter how good your intentions are.

The same applies to social media. You may be the nicest person in the world, but when you aren't familiar with the platform's culture, your behavior may come across as annoying or salesy.

Just like in real life, the fastest way to sync with the culture is to start doing what others do. Many rules are unwritten; you won't learn them by reading articles and watching tutorials, but by being present, observing other users, and emulating their behavior. The sooner you get your feet wet, the sooner you'll fit in with the "natives." Luckily, social media tend to be intuitive, and it shouldn't take more than a few days to acclimate yourself.

In the social media world, culture includes:

- The lingo: each platform has its own language.

- The technical side of things: how to set up your profile and use the platform.

- The type of content: format, length, topic, a point of view, and tone.

- Publishing frequency: how often to publish.

- Publishing and sharing ethics: how and when to share other people's content.

- Connecting with people: whom you can connect with.

- Communication: whom you can contact and how.

- Selling and self-promotion ethics: the ideal ratio of other people's content vs. your own and free advice vs. selling (if allowed at all).

- The platform's particularities.

Your success on social media depends on how well you understand the culture and also on your strategy, the value you share, and the way you interact with people. Below are a few universal tips, applicable on most social media platforms.

Serve before you sell

Social media aren't intended for selling, but for meeting people, having fun, and learning from each other. You always have to serve, help, educate, entertain, and connect before you ask for something.

Be relevant

To make your content relevant, interesting, and powerful, have a particular person in mind — your dream client — and adjust every piece of content to them.

Would they enjoy reading a 300-word post about a nightmare client session you had earlier that day? Would they love that kitten video compilation? That funny meme? Check everything with your dream client in your head before you post.

Be a curator

Sharing only content that you've created yourself is not just time-consuming; on many, if not most, social media platforms, it's considered spammy. Depending on the platform, 80% or more of *all* the content you share should be someone else's.

That's good news, isn't it? By sharing other people's content, you save a lot of time and energy while still adding value. And, as a bonus, it helps you build and strengthen relationships with other business owners. It's a win-win-win: for your audience, the person who created the content, and also for you.

Don't forget that your business accounts shouldn't feature content that *you* find interesting; curate for your dream client.

Be social

Social media automation tools and the demand for consistently adding value turn many people into link-sharing robots. Don't get us wrong here: curating links to relevant and useful content is not cheating, and neither is automation. But being on social media still must include being *social*. What does that mean?

• Engage with people one-on-one. Reach out to people (in line with the platform's culture) and be approachable and responsive when someone reaches out to you.

• Join communities. Many platforms have a community feature that enables you to join groups formed around a common interest. Groups are the best place to network, find collaboration partners, learn about your audience, and look for clients. Keep in mind that each community has its own internal culture and laws, both written and unwritten.

Be human

The fact that you are a small personal brand is your advantage. People want to interact with people, not abstract entities. That's why, instead of emulating big brands, you should bring forth your personality and your humanity. Here are some tips:

• In your profile pictures, show your face. Don't hide your identity behind a logo.

• In your bios, don't speak about yourself in the third person or in the plural (unless your business includes two or more people).

• Don't automate everything. Scheduling tools are helpful, but you can't automate your personality. Show up and engage with people.

• Take people behind-the-scenes, show work in progress, and share personal stories. Don't put filters on everything in the fear that someone would see you are imperfect.

- Whatever you share, talk to one person (your dream client), not to a nameless crowd.

- Use video (where applicable). There is no better way to show that you are real.

Be intentional

Plan your posts in advance so you can see the big picture of your social media strategy and batch your tasks. Come up with new content, mix it up with repurposed and other people's content, and schedule it (or have someone schedule it for you) so you can rest assured that there will *always* be signs of life on your social media.

This way, you can free up time to engage with people, be helpful, and have fun.

Chapter 4
Build a Blog That Matters

To make yourself visible online, you need to build a platform—a "soap box" you can step on so that others can see and hear you. A platform is your opportunity to market your brand in a humanized way—by educating, entertaining, and engaging your audience. It's a way to attract your dream clients, gain trust, position yourself as an expert, and make an impact.

Building a stable platform takes time; it won't happen overnight. However, by working the smart way, you can save a lot of time and frustration. That's what this chapter is all about.

Do you need to blog?

The chapter is called *Build a Blog That Matters*, but your platform doesn't have to be a traditional blog (a website where you regularly publish articles). If you've just felt a sense of relief, here are some alternatives for you to consider:

• a podcast

• a video channel

• a live show (a regular video or audio session that happens in real time)

• microblogging on social media (an equivalent of traditional blogging, but taking place on social media)

• visual storytelling on social media (the same as above, but using visual content)

• ultimate resources (a regular but infrequent release of in-depth guides, such as e-books and webinars)

The option you choose depends on your preferred ways of teaching and connecting with people, your audience's preferences and habits, and the purpose of your efforts (see the next section).

The following tips apply to any platform. Here, we use the word "blogging" to refer to any way of consistently sharing value.

Building a platform that matters: start with *why*

The reason many bloggers fail is that they blog without a clear purpose. Building a platform takes time, and not seeing results is frustrating. But knowing your *why* helps you stick with blogging through thick and thin.

You should be clear about the **chief purpose of your blog**. What's your business model? What role does the blog play in it? Do you want to monetize the content itself, or do you want to use it to market your services and products?

What do your people need from you? Is it education, motivation, tools, or something else? Do you need to build a large audience or a small, cozy community of loyal fans?

You also need to define **your core message**. *Why* do you do what you do? What is the thing you believe in so much that you're willing to opt out of the comfort of the *real job* into the unknown? Your *why* is the foundation of your business. And "to make money" is a weak and shaky foundation. To build a blog and business that matters, you need to dig much deeper.

Your *why* is also the main, often unconscious, reason certain people get attracted to you.

In the journal, you'll find some reflection questions to help you find your core message.

Work smart

Inconsistency and randomness are your enemies. Here is how to strike back:

• Come up with content ideas in advance and organize them in an editorial calendar (something as simple as a spreadsheet). Batch your tasks and work ahead of schedule.

• Make your paid services and products work together with your free content. Your free posts can be a part of the path to a paid product or service, a way to create a sense of urgency so that people want to buy, a way to test your ideas, or something you repurpose into a paid product or service later.

• Structure your content so that you motivate people to join your inner circle (usually an email list—the safest place to direct people to) or buy from you. Note: it's easier to make them commit in a small way first—such as asking for their email address—and slowly build trust rather than asking them to buy on the "first date."

• Make your social media channels work together with your blog. Don't overwhelm yourself and your readers by creating unique content for each of your channels. Communicate the same messages in slightly different ways, link to your main platform, and vice versa.

Stick to your niche

It may seem that talking about everything under the sun is easier than limiting yourself to a narrow topic. But, in fact, staying focused helps you:

• go deeper, as opposed to scratching the surface and sharing generic advice

- come up with creative, impactful, and useful content

- build a loyal following and meaningful relationships

- save time and energy

- position yourself as an expert

- become an expert — because, with every piece of content, you learn more about the topic

- be more profitable (as a result of everything above)

Talk to your ideal client

The main difference between business blogging and any other kind of writing you may have done, like academic or fiction writing, is that business blogging starts from a place of empathy with your reader.

Your success depends on your ability to stand in your ideal client's shoes. That's why you need to have a *particular* person in mind when you write, preferably (but not necessarily) someone you know, and talk directly to them.

When you talk to your ideal client, you can share from the heart. Instead of lecturing them, you engage them in a heart-to-heart conversation. Just like when chatting with a friend, you can be relaxed, vulnerable, and unapologetically yourself. And *that* is what makes your readers fall in love with you — or not.

You have to take the risk, because if you insist on writing for and being liked by everyone, your blog remains soulless.

Chapter 5
Craft a Website That Works for You

Your website can be a hardworking employee who never sleeps and always looks her best. While *you* sleep or mind your own business, she makes sure that every dream client who visits your online space feels welcomed and gets what they came for.

But she can also turn out to be a saboteur who repels and confuses people.

If the latter is true, don't worry. It's not too hard to fix. And if you have no online space at all, it's time to get started building one.

Let's talk about how to make your website

work *for* you, not against you.

11 elements of a professional, legit website

First of all, you need to show people that *you* are real and that *your business* is real. Here are the elements you need to have in place:

1. Your own domain.

2. Obligatory static pages: homepage, about page, blog, services, contact. You don't have to name the pages this way, but people *are* looking for them, and if they don't find them in five seconds, they may leave.

3. A professional photo of yourself. Faces build trust, and photos show your clients that you're real. Place a photo *at least* on the about page.

4. Your real, full name. In case the name of your business is different from your name, make sure your name is somewhere on your website (ideally the about page and/or contact page), and that people can find it. Your name is what makes you a real, trustworthy person who has nothing to hide.

5. Your location. In the online world, geography isn't relevant, right? Or is it? Your location supports the feeling that you're a real person with a real, offline life.

6. A signup form.

7. A privacy policy and terms and conditions.

8. Social proof. People will trust you only if they see that *other people* trust you. You can show them by displaying testimonials, case studies, awards, logos of websites that have featured your articles, or at least — if you're just getting started and don't have any of these yet — links to active social media.

9. Links to *active* and *professional* social media profiles.

10. Your contact information. Tell people how they can contact you (give them at least two options) and why they should.

11. Pricing. Share your prices proudly, openly, and visibly.

Make your copy clear and powerful

Every element of your website should focus on one thing so that your website visitors won't get confused or paralyzed by choice. Here is what to do:

• For each page on your website, define *one* main purpose: Why is this page here? To create a deeper connection with your readers (about page)? To show your expertise (blog)? Consider the bigger picture of your online presence and your business as such. Think about the value — what's in it for your dream client? Why should they care?

• Then, define *one* specific objective for each of the pages: sell your offer (sales page), make first-time visitors subscribe to your newsletter (homepage), make people who are already interested in you schedule a free consultation (contact page), and so on. The difference between a purpose (point #1) and an objective is that an objective is actionable: it refers to what you want people to *do* after they read the page. Think about one thing for each page — even if it's just to go to another page of your website. Not all pages have to sell or convert subscribers, but all pages should contain a call to action. A single and clear call to action.

• Turn the objective into a call to action: e.g., join my list, schedule a lesson, fill in the form. Be creative here — "subscribe" doesn't inspire people to take action.

• Remove everything that doesn't support the main objective.

Building an online presence from scratch is a battle with your inner critic and your fears. We've all been there. In the beginning, it may seem impossible to talk about yourself and what you do in a loud, proud voice.

But people who come to you aren't looking for your demons; they're looking for help. And they want to be assured that they've found the right person.

Here is how to make your words confident and powerful so that people can trust you:

• Talk to your dream client. Address every word to them. This is also the best way to conquer your fears — talking into the darkness is difficult and scary.

- Stay away from general, meaningless, and vague phrases. Don't use words you can see on other people's websites or words that everyone uses. We become blind to the words that we see too often.

- Be specific. Your students' stories, your own stories, your why—that's what makes your copy confident, persuasive, unique, and attractive.

- Weed out redundant, empty, and weak words. Make every sentence and every word count. Replace complex words and jargon. Don't use words a typical member of your audience wouldn't use. The plainer the language, the better.

- Improve organization. Web copy isn't crime fiction—don't save the best for last. Place the most important information at the top of the page, and put the most important words at the beginning of the sentences.

- Improve readability. Use large fonts, white

space, simple words, short sentences, short paragraphs, subheads, bullet points, and bold text for emphasis.

A few words about web design

You don't need to pay hundreds of dollars for web design. Not when you're just getting started, anyway. Investing a big amount of money in design before you get started working with real people and before you gain clarity about your brand isn't smart.

In the beginning, all you need is a minimalist website template, a color palette (one main color and a few supporting ones that work together well), and one font. Keep things simple and consistent. Your web visitors will appreciate it more than they would a festival of gimmicks.

Chapter 6
Develop an Outstanding Personal Brand

What do you imagine when you hear the word "brand"? If you're like most people, the first thing that pops into your mind is a logo and maybe a tagline. But branding goes much deeper. It is much more than a disposable surface layer of your business.

According to Seth Godin, a brand is "the set of expectations, memories, stories and relationships that, taken together, account for a consumer's decision to choose one product or service over another."[i]

What does it mean for people who want to teach online? And do you *need* a brand?

As an online teacher or coach, you have two options: You can work for established brands—marketplaces that connect you with your clients—or you can go independent and create your own brand.

Working for big brands has many advantages:

• They provide you a place to "live" online so you don't have to build a website.

• They take care of marketing so you don't have to pay for ads, create your own content, or build an email list.

• They bring you visibility and clients so you can concentrate on teaching or coaching.

But because you're reading this book, you'd probably prefer developing your own brand—which is what we suggest doing—over working under someone else's brand, especially when the "someone" is not a person, but a company.

Why you need a brand

Why should you opt out of the comfortable option and choose the harder path of building your own brand? There are three main reasons.

1. Your expertise and personality are unique.

The expertise and personality you bring to the table are not interchangeable with those of other professionals and shouldn't be treated as a commodity, which is exactly what happens on online teaching platforms. When you sell your services through a big marketplace, you're just one of many. Your prices, the way your customers value your time and expertise, the way you value your own skills—it all reflects the commodity mindset.

2. When you work for someone else, your clients aren't yours.

You never know what may happen to the platform or how its conditions may change in the future. In fact, from the long-term perspective, playing on your own ground is safer than working for a big platform. Without your own clients on your own email list, you can lose everything in one day, when the platform changes its business model or even goes out of business. Unless you're the one who is in charge, you never know what's going on behind the scenes.

3. A brand is what connects you with your audience on a deeper level.

Through a personal brand, you have a chance to attract people who share your values and your worldview. There is no ceiling on the number of people whose lives you can impact in a meaningful way and who can help you make your vision a reality.

In summary, if you want to build a smart and sustainable living online, and if you want to make an impact, you need your own brand.

Brand management

Where exactly does "developing your brand" start? When you come up with a tagline? Launch your website? Decide on your brand logo and colors? When you make the first sale? No. It's much sooner.

The moment you take the leap and venture into an online business, you *become* a personal brand—whether you try or not. Following Seth Godin's definition, with every step you take and every word you say online, you create "expectations, memories, stories and relationships" that make your products and services more or less attractive.

So, to be precise, the question isn't how to develop a brand, but how to *manage* it so that a particular client—your ideal client—chooses you over someone else.

Brand management starts with positioning: What people imagine when they think about your brand. Because it's your audience's interpretation of your brand that counts, not yours.

When you position yourself well, you reserve a spot for your brand in your audience's mind, so that whenever they hear or think about a specific thing (your expertise), they think about you.

A step-by-step guide to positioning your personal brand

1. Be very clear about your *why* and *how*. This is why you do what you do and what sets you apart. It's your special sauce and your personality.

2. Zero in on a specific group of people with a specific problem (a niche). Find your *who* and *what*.

3. Start building your online presence (website,

blog, email list, social media, communities). Everything you do and say online from now on should be in alliance with your *why*, aimed at your ideal client, and centred around the problem you solve for them.

Stay focused and get rid of everything that doesn't fit into the picture you're painting.

4. Build your design arsenal: a simple, letter-based logo, a color palette, one font, a clean website template, and templates for your images.

The thing is, if you put all the work into positioning your brand and forget about visual branding, the image in your audience's mind remains hazy. By being intentional and consistent with your visuals, you, quite literally, give your brand a shape and a color and help people remember you.

5. Start solving the problem for *real* people. That's how you build your portfolio and social proof and make it clear that you are able to

solve the problem.

From now on, when sharing your portfolio, show only the kind of work you want to do. It might be tempting to share testimonials or content you created before you niched down, but you have to resist the temptation and stay focused. If you have nothing niche-related to share yet, start creating blog and social media posts, free consultations, webinars and e-books. Everything adds to your portfolio.

6. Promote your work, connect with people, and provide value. Stay focused and consistent so that each piece of your online presence, no matter how big or small, fits into the big picture of your brand.

Please use the exercises in the Journal to gain clarity about your brand.

Chapter 7
Detect Your Ideal Client

When we first start working online, most of us teachers and coaches apply only one client selection filter: our client is anyone who pays.

Sooner or later, we notice that the "money filter" lets in all kinds of clients. Some of them are a breeze to work with, and their results knock your socks off, whereas others seem to be change-resistant, no matter how much time and energy you invest in them.

But you continue working with everyone, because the idea of saying no to a paying client is unimaginable. So you suffer through client calls that make you about as excited as a dentist appointment and pray not to get another client of this kind again.

Here's the harsh truth: prayers won't help. You need to opt out of your deeply rooted *real job* mindset and think like an entrepreneur. Because you don't become an entrepreneur the day you get your first paying client, but the day you turn down a paying client for the first time — without feeling bad about it.

The quest for an ideal client

Earlier in the book, we made the point that teachers and coaches have a hard time saying no because of their natural desire to help people. But the "I want to help everyone" attitude isn't the only mindset that needs shifting.

There are many beliefs and habits adapted from the *real job* culture that you may take for granted and that have no place in the smart online business world. To name some of them:

7 Detect Your Ideal Client

- The more clients, the better.

- Giving up on a client is lazy and cowardly.

- Saying no to a paying client is saying no to money.

- I'm here to serve people, and refusing to help is self-centered.

- Work isn't supposed to be fun. I can't fire a client just because I don't like them.

Here's the thing: by living by these and similar rules, you are doing your clients no favors. In fact, your martyrdom doesn't help anyone. Your bad-fit clients cost you a lot of time, energy, and sanity. As a result, you have too little to offer *everyone* who works with you.

The first step in the quest for a dream client is to challenge your *real job* mindset and understand that choosing whom you work with is not just possible; it's necessary. It's not self-centered; it's thoughtful. It's not lazy and cowardly; it's harder than saying yes to everyone. And also smarter.

Who is your ideal client?

The second step in the quest for a dream client is to establish criteria for an excellent client fit. These should include:

• **Your niche.** The person has to fall into the specific group you defined earlier and find themselves at the point when they experience the problem you're solving.

• **Essential qualities of your ideal client.** In your world, what does it mean when someone is a good client? What kind of people do you enjoy working with? And what kind of people enjoy working with you?

- **Your current goals and priorities.** Do you have the mental space and time to work with the client right now?

In the journal, you'll find a worksheet to help you establish your criteria.

How to repel bad-fit clients before it's too late

When you're just starting out, you may be more liberal about the people you work with. Later, as your clientele grows, you can apply more filters. But you should always be in control of who can work with you directly and protect yourself from nightmare and toxic clients, as well as people who are a bad fit for you.

Here is how to do it:

- **Define a bad-fit client.** Just like with a dream

client, get clear about what it means when someone is a bad fit. What kind of people don't click with you? What are their habits, attitudes, and values? Make a list of traits.

• **Say it out loud.** In your copy, be explicit about who your services and products are *not* intended for. Include a "this is not for you if" section on your services page and sales pages.

• **Make no premature commitments.** Because people who aren't a good fit for most teachers and coaches are also people who tend not to read sales pages carefully, make sure no one can get in your door without your approval. Have application forms or discovery calls in place. Ask strategic questions that help you spot a bad-fit client.

• **Say no, but don't let them leave empty-handed.** Saying no is a lot easier when you can offer an alternative solution. Sending the person to someone you know who you think is a better fit feels good because it helps everyone involved—provided the client is just a bad fit for you, not a toxic or nightmare client. But even if you can't or don't want to transfer the person to someone else, you can still recommend useful resources like books or online courses (your own or someone else's).

• **Protect yourself (and your clients).** Having a service agreement in place helps you establish healthy client relationships and create a space where everyone feels safe.

How to break up with clients

If you don't have any advanced selection criteria in place, there's a good chance you're dealing with a few bad fits. Letting them go isn't easy, but it's necessary because you need to make room for your dream clients.

Here are some tips:

- **Get rid of the nightmare clients first.** Working with nightmare clients is taking a toll on your productivity, energy level, creativity, love for your work, quality of your work, and even your health. Finish what you have to finish and say goodbye to them as soon as you can.

- **Raise your prices.** Increasing your rates solves the problem for you because it makes all less-than-ideal clients quit.

- **Offer an alternative.** Again, when sending your clients away, tell them where to go. Transfer them to someone else or recommend a helpful resource.

How to attract dream clients

Now, you may be wondering how to attract the right kind of people and make them want to work with you or buy from you. The fact is, you already know how to do that. In the previous chapters, where we talked about changing your mindset, niching down, connecting with people through social media and your own platform, building a website, and positioning your brand—all of this together helps your dream clients find you and get to know, like, and trust you.

Chapter 8
Hack Your Pricing (Hint: It's Not About Money)

"How much do you charge an hour?"

Once you move into running an online business where "all the money is," one of the first questions you'll ask is how much to charge. Do you charge more or less than face-to-face? Do you look around and strike your own average? Do you find out what people can afford and go from there?

The real question shouldn't be how much to charge. The deeper question is always, "**Why do I charge this much?**" Then you realize that it's really not about the price tag, but about your confidence level and your positioning.

But let's start from the beginning and see why **online sessions** may seem undervalued, and why you should never think that if you work "online" you have to artificially lower your prices.

Is online training worth as much as live training?

There are several myths associated with the value of online training.

Myth #1: You can't charge as much because you're online and don't spend money on transportation to and from work.

It's a valid point, but it's not entirely true. In fact, if anything, you should be comfortable charging *more* for the convenience your *clients* experience by not spending time in traffic.

Think of restaurants, for instance. When you eat out, you *pay for the convenience* of someone preparing and setting the food directly in front of you. And don't forget that a convenient and easy-to-use gadget will cost you more than a bulky machine.

Working online helps your client save time. When your clients save time, they have more opportunities to make money, so anything that saves time and is more convenient has a higher value.

Myth #2: Working with clients online doesn't require textbooks and other investments, so it should cost less.

While you might not require your clients to purchase expensive books, you do spend time looking for relevant materials for the session. On top of that, there might be expenses associated with running the business and making your sessions smooth and your client's experience worthwhile. You may be investing in conference call or scheduling software, website development, or even accounting software, and this all has to be a part of your pricing decision making.

Unlike traditional classrooms, teaching online is more than just teaching. You're running an online business, which means that sometimes your mind is occupied with more than just programs and plans.

So the decisions you make as a business owner are usually impacted by a larger perspective, which may mean you say no to some projects (even if it means saying no to immediate money) in favor of those that bring you closer to your goals.

Why do you charge this much?

This is the best question to ask when it comes to pricing decisions, because as a business owner, **your pricing speaks of your brand.** Apart from charging a certain amount to cover your overhead expenses, **there has to be value attachment** that your client will communicate as being worthwhile (or not).

What does that mean exactly?

Niche product and focus on value

It's hard to justify charging higher amounts if what you're offering is pretty much the same as what everyone else. If that's the case, then your only difference from your competition is indeed price.

Niching down not only relieves you of the stressful pleasing game; it makes you an expert, and by default your products and services become unique.

It doesn't mean that all of a sudden you need to spike your prices. That's not the goal here. Knowing your niche, however, will help you find the most suitable format that will give your client the best results and allow you to teach fewer hours but still charge for the **valuable services you provide.**

For instance, say you teach business communication skills. The conventional method is to have one-on-one sessions in which you share what you know with your client. Instead, try creating a "flipped" experience where all you do is provide guidance, and your clients develop their business communication skills by reading material selected by you, organizing vocabulary lists (following your tips), writing reviews, and sending recordings with their own summaries.

Then you charge per package of services based on the value (i.e., results) the client receives after taking your program. It's unconventional but much more effective for the client, because, as we know, until the clients "get their hands dirty," they won't develop the skills they need.

By knowing your niche, you create a unique product/service that doesn't have to be priced "per hour." Rather, its price will be **determined by value.**

Know your competition

Your first impulse in your online business might be to compete based on price. You want to charge *less* than your competition, which doesn't communicate the value your brand brings.

If the majority of entrepreneurs are basing their

pricing on a number, consider choosing a different marker for your services. Think of Apple products, for example. They don't have to lower their price, because they've chosen a different dimension that makes them stand out: beauty.

While all other computers are trying to outdo others based on price, Apple's brand loyalty is high because they position themselves as the brand with the most pleasing design.

Think outside the pricing parameters to label your services and products as unique.

The question of "why do I charge this much?" is more powerful because it gets you to focus on **the benefits your client will receive.** And as you narrow down your focus and begin crafting specific packages, even changing the format of instruction, you'll gain more confidence charging differently and pricing yourself beyond your competition.

Chapter 9
Get Your First Clients Online

Client work is the fastest, safest (low risk), and easiest way to bring cash into your business. Yet, it's naive to expect clients to find us on their own. They won't just "stumble" on our website, which has thirty page views a day.

When you begin working online, finding clients seems daunting. You feel alone and crushed by the weight of the newly discovered entrepreneurial modus operandi: hustling.

It might sound counterintuitive, but to find clients, you first need to discover yourself. It's going back to the idea of the necessary mindset change, the transformation that will make the "new software" work. Consider these three aspects to help you mold yourself and make finding clients more successful:

1) your core message

2) your visibility

3) befriending an influencer

Also, get used to the idea that it won't happen on day one. Most new entrepreneurs struggle with finding clients, and the confidence to offer your services is built over a period of time. Just like with learning a language, you don't become fluent overnight.

Chiseling your message and *narrowing* your focus will get you more clients than teaching yourself all the tricks in the book, finding new training, and adding to your résumé so you can serve *any* client. In real life, it's the opposite: coaches and teachers take extra courses to diversify their portfolios, instead of cutting out the extras so their potential clients can see whether they will work together.

It's easier to add than to reduce. Adding is mindless. It's like hoarding recognition items to heal insecurity. Reducing, on the other hand, takes work and sweat. Not everyone is prepared to do that. Perhaps this explains why we would rather get an extra license than dig deeper into our core message.

#1: Finding your core message

Loyal clients are the ones who are attracted to more than the look of your website. They sync with your *why*.

What is the irreducible minimum of your services? What do you seek to accomplish? What results do you want for your clients and *why*? This is your core message: a line that *must come through* in every piece of content you share.

Now go back to your website and social media to see how well your core message shows. It doesn't have to be "pretty," but it has to be **clear and focused.** You also need to take away the elements that may confuse people.

#2: Increasing your visibility

We find it ironic that people who choose to work online (especially teachers moving out of a traditional classroom) want to have nothing to do with social media. The number of times online teachers have expressed they want to avoid social media at all costs is evidence that the problem isn't unique.

It's not that your business can't exist without social media. Alexandra Franzen closed her Twitter account, and that didn't affect her client intake.[ii] But Franzen was already a successful writer by the time she decided to stop fretting over her social media presence. Plus her email list is strong enough that she doesn't need to be "more visible."

When your business is online, social media is one of the ways to create visibility — not just for yourself, but also to make yourself known to other people with greater influence online.

Another note: social media isn't for finding clients. It's for building your visibility and making people aware of your brand. Don't assume that just by tweeting five times a day your clients will come knocking at the door. But just as a marriage relationship starts with a casual chat, your client relationship begins on social media, so you can't ignore it.

Finally, social media loves strategy. You may be sharing something useful ten times a day, but if you don't have an overall strategy that shows where every piece of the puzzle goes, your efforts will be in vain.

Think of the next step that intensifies your core message. Once people decide they like the core message, you can't leave them there. There has to be an action step, even if it's as "small" as people sharing your piece of content or giving you their email address.

#3: Befriending an influencer

There's likely someone in your industry whom you admire and want to emulate. Generally, this person's influence isn't far out of reach, but they're a few years ahead of you on the business journey you're about to start.

If you **genuinely** like their work and want to learn, they might be able to help you. Here are some of the ways you can get acquainted with the influencer in your industry:

- Follow this person on social media and take note of what they're sharing.

- Like/share their content *if you like it.*

- Join online support groups.

- Buy this person's book or course and leave a review.

- Send an email with your *genuine* reflection of their work.

- Interview this person on your blog.

Some important notes: These are all ideas; use what's applicable. Also, don't contact the person unless you *genuinely like* their work. Phoney emails are easy to spot, so if you feel like you're not sure, don't do it. Wait until you find someone whose work you admire.

Finally, it won't take long before you realize that you, too, can help others. You may not be the greatest influencer of all time or be able to brag about your six-figure income, but in a small way you will be able to help someone.

If you want to become an influencer, start today. Write. Share what others write. Get over your fears and insecurities. There are too many people pushing their agendas for you to sit quietly in the corner and pretend you're not ready to share anything online yet.

Change your mindset

Just like many other chapters, this one is about changing your mindset. It's a critical step in your online business journey, as tactics without substance are empty tricks that will make you look exactly like what you don't want: salesy, desperate, and "like everyone else."

Begin working on the above three essential mindset-changing strategies, along with the practical exercises in your Journal, and the results will follow.

Chapter 10
Find Money to Invest in Yourself

Imagine teaching at a prestigious school where all of your needs are met, your schedule is flexible, and you have the most diligent students. Imagine the excitement of your boss over your next innovative idea. Imagine the support you'd get from the staff and all the perks that come with it.

Finding such an environment is unlikely to happen, and if you do find it, it's highly unlikely that you would quit. After all, when your schedule is flexible and your financial and emotional needs are met, why would you opt out?

When you join the online business world, think of your environment like this: there's flexibility and freedom, the boss (you) is excited about your projects, and there's tremendous reward for doing what you're passionate about. Yet many people quit within their first year.

The main reason is money. Generating income is a chore that online entrepreneurs aren't prepared to tackle. They imagine their online business the same way they do a traditional job: you get a job, you find clients, but then *someone else* is taking care of you.

The last part is where it all goes wrong, because online professionals aren't always prepared to call themselves what they now are: business owners.

When it comes to money, here's what separates a professional from a business owner:

• A professional looks at all the money made **as personal income (salary)**

- A business owner looks at all the money made as total business revenue (making salary an expense).

When you take multiple courses on how to run a business online, this basic but crucial distinction never comes up. According to these courses, all you need to do is find clients, make money, and draw your salary.

Never mind setting aside money for training, masterminding, or coaching. With this mindset, you can't even afford books. That's the sad reality of imposing an online business format on professionals who don't see themselves as online business owners.

No wonder the dropout rate is so high.

In our Opted Out community on Facebook, we asked online teachers how much money they invest in their businesses. The overwhelming majority answered that they "don't have the money" to invest.

But this tendency doesn't change when they get money. Again, we have to attack the mindset. The same online teacher who treats business revenue as a "for me to spend" allowance will never have enough to invest in their business unless they change something in the very beginning.

While with a traditional teaching position, for instance, investment becomes an add-on or a luxury, **it is a *must* with an online business.**

Clarifying "investment"

Another challenge is that the word "investment" has gained a bad rap by being used out of context. Online teachers these days say things like:

"I've *invested* in an email marketing service."

10 Find Money to Invest in Yourself

"I've *invested* in a new camera and lighting."

"I've *invested* in new software to help me with bookkeeping."

Because they tend to "invest" in these things, they don't consider education and coaching as a worthy investment, or they think of it as something they will invest in some day in the future.

It's important to understand that **you can't invest in something that depreciates.** So no matter how cool your new headset is, it's **not an investment** but a **liability** that can fall apart the next day.

Software and monthly subscriptions cannot be categorized as investments either, because they are overhead expenses. If you need them to run your business, you don't *invest* in them; you just *buy* them.

Investment is something you purchase to see it appreciate in the long-term future. Business owners can purchase real estate, stocks, and shares as an investment, but when you begin your online business, there are two types of investment that will appreciate over time:

• Investment in your own business (creating products/services that will *continue selling* through your website).

• Investment in education.[iii]

Investment strategy for online teachers

To invest and grow, you need to *redesign* your business structure. You can no longer draw 100% (minus taxes or other payments) as your salary. The rule of thumb is that you draw roughly 50% of all of your earnings as your salary, leaving 50% in the business.

The 50% you leave in the business is the money you use to pay taxes, overhead costs, and any employees. It's also what you use to invest back in the business (website improvement, ads, marketing) and invest in education and training.

You're probably wondering right now how to double up on everything you're already doing, but if your plate is full as it is, doubling up won't help. It will exhaust you and won't bring you the results you want.

The main principle in redesigning your business in a smart way is to begin freeing up your time. How can you train the same number of clients, make the same amount of money, and spend only half the time working with them?

Consider these options:

• Create an environment where your clients do more work.

- Create a format in which you will be needed only as a guide.

- Design a program in which your students have more freedom and fewer one-on-one time.

- Structure a part of your training as a video/audio course that will reduce your one-on-one hours.

Once you envision this program, create a pilot and run it. Use your creativity and expertise to convince your clients that they can learn only when they invest their own time, not use yours.

Freeing up time is a process that involves education, creativity, and entrepreneurial skills, but once you begin thinking differently, changes will happen within months.

After that is done, identify a program/course *you* want to be a part of, and write down why and how this investment will produce a return. Beware of enrolling in something on a whim for the sake of potentially making a lot of money without a plan in place.

For instance, if you've been teaching exam prep, the best investment will be to learn how you can do it more efficiently. Don't invest in a neurological coaching school just because they promised you can charge $200 an hour after you're done.

Develop what you already have, and build on it to get the return. If you're not sure what you know or what you might need to learn, invest in a coach. You will be amazed how fast you'll be moving (and how much support you'll receive) once you work with someone who understands what running an online business is like.

Chapter 11
Create a Small, Actionable, and Sellable Online Course

Everyone seems to be creating an online course these days. Making something that sells consistently is a challenge, though. It's a sale (followed by repeat sales) that speaks of the product's success, and the ability to do that doesn't happen on a first try.

When authors package their expertise and put it online, there are two things they struggle with the most:

1) narrowing down the topic (the core of the course)

2) keeping it small, simple, and actionable

What's the core of your course?

In her blog post on course creation[iv], Breanne Dyck said this of course creators:

"So used to thinking about their course from the perspective of what they know, they find that they're unable to break free and really pay attention to what their customers think they want. And when we try to think like our customers, we end up falling victim to the curse of expertise.

Unable to truly adopt a beginner's mind, we overcomplicate things."

According to Dyck, there are five fundamental reasons anyone would consider when buying a course, and ironically, they have nothing to do with the course topic. Universally, all people want to hear from an expert because they want to:

1) save time,

2) make money,

3) save energy,

4) save (or not lose) money now or in the future,

5) feel better about themselves.

For instance, we might think that our clients want a course that will teach them specific sets of exercising routines, but what they really want is to learn how to exercise and stay fit (feel better about themselves) without spending hours at the gym (save time).

We may think that our clients want a course that will teach them how to use grammar, but in fact our clients want to spend less time learning grammar and still speak well (feel better about themselves).

How to nail your client's exact "pain"

To uncover our client's pain, we need to start with what our clients think they need, not what we think we can give them. This is a crucial distinction that will either make your course into an incredible transformational experience or cause your course to contribute to the general noise.

The easiest way to nail down your customer's pain is to interact with them and get to know what struggles they face. The mistake we make is to assume there's only one way to find that out: a survey. But there are different ways of going about it. Here are some ideas:

• Asking a question on a forum. (Don't preface it with "I'm creating a course and have to do the market analysis." Just *ask* a specific question.)

• Writing emails to some of your most active

subscribers (ask them, if there was one thing they could learn from you, what it would be and why).

- Paying attention to the comments to your blog posts, videos, and podcasts.

- Paying attention to what your *potential customers* are saying by reading related product/course reviews, forum questions, and random comments[v].

Once you begin paying attention, you will be taking extensive notes and discovering some things that you never thought your customers needed. You can also connect it to your personal experience (where it applies) and go back to being a beginner, which most "experts" forget how to do after they learn something.

How do you make it small?

Don't think you're done once you've nailed down the pain, because you have another huge monster to face. The gremlin you will be tackling next is volume.

Generally, teachers have no problem making a three-hundred-page manual and thirty one-hour videos for a course. It's the customers who have issues going through it.

Reducing the volume of content to a small and actionable minimum is a must when you decide to craft an incredible learning experience. Somehow we think we're cheating our audience out of their money if we create ten ten-minute video tutorials and ten one-page worksheets instead of hour-long productions with voluminous manuals.

"But I have to make sure they know," goes the all-too-familiar tune. Yet, the customers don't just want knowledge; they want to apply the knowledge so that it changes their lives *now*.

Make it easy for them to go through your materials and apply the concepts right away.

Here are the steps to take if you wish to reduce your volume:

• Choose **one pain** that persists from comments and surveys.

• Ask yourself **why** the person struggles with it.

• Develop **steps** to help this person **overcome the pain** (here's a place to show your expertise).

• Make explanations small, simple, and clear.

• Add actionable content.

For instance, your customer struggles with finding time to exercise. Obviously, they need to know how to exercise, but that's not the pain. The pain is not being able to find the time.

That, in turn, will make you adjust your content

to help your customer, first, plan their time and, second, choose the routines that will be most effective while being less time-consuming. Maybe you'll want to encourage them to exercise throughout the day as an option and adopt a "life as an exercise" motto?

How do you keep it actionable?

The best way to keep it actionable is to create *actionable content*. Here are some characteristics of actionable content (check out Breanne Dyck's book[vi] to get deeper):

• Keep your tutorials short (ten to fifteen minutes).

• Add worksheets and workbooks with questions and real-life application tips.

• Add tracking sheets to help participants go

11 Create an Online Course

back and analyze their progress.

- Facilitate feedback, make it easily accessible, and format it differently.

- Develop metrics to assess progress.

Making it actionable can be a challenge for you, as the focus shifts from what *you* want to include in the course to what *your customer* really needs. The process forces you to step over your "curse of knowledge" and think like a beginner.

Actionable content makes your learner autonomous, so the goal of any course is for your participants to no longer need you because they can navigate the world on their own.

Chapter 12
Delegate to Work Smarter

"We've got so much to do and so little time that the idea of spending time doing anything unrelated to the to-do list actually creates stress. ... We even convince ourselves that sleep is a terrible use of our time." Brené Brown.

It won't take you long to discover that there are not enough hours in the day to complete everything on your to-do list. In fact, you might do yourself a great service if you tell yourself that you'll never complete *everything* on your to-do list, and that's OK.

Teaching online is more than teaching, and many people start out alone. They don't sleep, they eat junk for days (or skip meals), and they proudly tell their friends they've done

everything on their own. They end up treating their bodies like machines that can function when told. Until they break.

This is a controversial chapter that may sound appalling and too "radical" for solopreneurs who wear their "busyness" as their badge of honor and frequently feel guilty about taking an afternoon off instead of hoarding tasks on their to-do lists. They feel like cheaters, impostors, and losers when they decide to hire someone, and most frequently they wait to hire anybody until they can afford it.

As it happens, they will never be able to afford to hire a team member because of wrong budgeting and an exhausted mind that runs on caffeine. They may reach a point when they actually needed to hire someone yesterday but won't be able to afford to spend money in the process of training someone. (That's the plight of some six-figure, self-made entrepreneurs.)

There are multiple systems you can incorporate

to make your work more efficient (including automation and apps), but the focus of this chapter is on delegation: how to go about it and how to make it work for you before you think you're "ready."

Projects you will need help with in the beginning

If you build your entire business around one-on-one services, it's hard to think of why you would hire anybody else. The intuitive decision is to hire "your clone" who can share your workload, but that means training them (usually free) without any guarantees of consistent employment.

Working for a marketplace where you offer your services alongside thousands of others doesn't make it easier to think of yourself as an entrepreneur. You need your own space, however small, to build your unique following and ultimately offer your services and products.

So let's first look at the most basic business elements that you may not be aware of working as a freelancer:

• marketing (social media, email, and content)

• product creation and sales (packaging your services and selling them)

• vision (knowing exactly where you're going: niche, client, and focus)

Vision

First is vision. You'll notice it's listed last above (because it's alphabetical), but this is exactly where the majority of entrepreneurs keep it, especially when daily chores overshadow it.

But imagine putting money into a website or even a landing page, only to discover later that your focus should have been something different. You change the niche or add new elements to your brand, and all of a sudden your website becomes old.

Most entrepreneurs invest in a website *before* they have a vision and a strategy for their business. It's like buying language learning books before you discover what is needed (and before you realize that you don't need *that many* books).

Investing in your vision is vital. It has to come before anything else, or as you grow your business selling your first services or packages. Most businesses fail in their first stages because they don't invest in their business vision. They have puzzle pieces in place (marketing, product creation, sales), but they don't know where everything is going and why.

So, hire a coach or a group of coaches, and book

a discovery session so you learn that the **goal of your business isn't just exchanging your hours for money.**

Marketing

Marketing is that element that keeps all the other pieces well-oiled and functioning. Marketing can be outsourced.

Here's what's included in it:

- social media

- email marketing

- content marketing (writing blog posts, creating videos or podcasts)

- advertising

Social media: This can be overwhelming, but not if you start with one social media channel. Depending on your audience needs, you can pick one that fits the best.

Email marketing: once people find you on social media and enjoy the content you share, they will want to connect with you more, so build a bridge from social media to email, and invite people to sign up for your newsletter.

Sending out regular updates and newsletters is the easiest way to build trust and convert consumers into customers. You can outsource the mechanics of setting up a newsletter too.

Content marketing: While nobody but you can create your unique content, you can hire people to do editing or formatting for you. Those tasks are time- and labor-intensive, and outsourcing them will help you work smarter and focus on sales.

Advertising: There are different ways to advertise your services, and not all of them have to be paid. The most efficient is guest-posting, and you need a strong network of people to make this work.

You can also invest in paid advertising, and banner ads would be your best bet for the money and the audience. Unlike with pay-per-click advertising, banner ads bring you warm audience, and you don't have to do much to learn the mechanics of setting up campaigns.

Whatever method of advertising you choose, you need help setting up regular campaigns or researching for new venues to find clients. Some of these tasks should be delegated.

Delegation workflow

First, single out the tasks you need help with. Write down a step-by-step process. For instance, for client onboarding, you need to set up an automated welcome email with a general description of your services, plus the terms and conditions document.

Second, create deadlines to track progress and check in with your assistant. Communicate via chat rather than email, as it's faster.

Finally, meet once a month to cast a vision and explain why and how certain things are done. Sharing a bigger picture helps an assistant know what part they play and how to play it.

Once you have a clear vision of the impact you're trying to make with your business, you'll be able to outline and outsource smaller tasks to free yourself for bigger projects that only you can do.

After some time, you will see your efforts paying off as you will be more efficient and prolific, while your team will be working behind the scenes to help you move forward faster.

Delegation succeeds when you're sure of your vision and you know exactly how to get there. By tackling one tedious task after another you will soon experience more creative and financial freedom.

Conclusion

The book we've written is the life we've lived. It may sound too good to be true, but because we've written this new chapter in our lives and made it a reality, we know you can too.

When teachers or coaches are overburdened with administrative responsibilities on top of their regular teaching schedules, they wonder if this is the only way online work is supposed to be: too many ill-fitting clients, too much hustle, too many hours spent working on things that aren't adding value long-term.

Desperate to find answers, they resolve to living like this, because in the big scheme of things, this still feels better than being hired by an obsessive and competitive university or a smaller company with little opportunity for growth.

Or, contrary to their personal convictions, they will resort to gimmicks and tricks, because how else can one succeed in this online business gig, right?

We've written this book to share with you how you can **opt out** of the self-imposed *real job* martyrdom, sleazy sales gimmicks, and strategies that go against your business vision, so you embrace *smart* online teaching that brings your creative best to the people who need it the most and rewards you financially without violating other people's freedom.

Opting out doesn't happen overnight, and you don't just wake up one day with all of your things sorted and quandaries resolved. But as you make daily conscious decisions that resonate with your personal brand manifesto, you *will* opt out of the *real job* mentality that keeps your business from making an impact only you can make.

We hope you found this book inspiring and motivational. Please connect with us by sending us your feedback on www.optedoutlife.com.

Yours,

Elena Mutonono & Veronika Palovska

Acknowledgements

We would like to thank our backers who "bought us coffee" and thus supported this work: Cara Leopold, Louise Robertson, Alexandra Kapinya, Maria Seco, Fern Kushner, Tania Maximenko, Barbara Rocci, Halima Reynolds, Kate Fisher, Maria Teresa Zoppello, Curt Ford, Elfin Waters, Samantha Dematagoda.

Elena

I would like to thank the larger Opted Out community for tuning in, sharing experiences, and supporting other online teachers. You are my motivation.

I'm grateful to my clients, program participants,

and *Smart Teacher's Library* members, whose contribution has enriched my coaching experience and sharpened my focus so they can teach smarter.

Thanks to Darius Foroux whose "real job" phrase in one of his posts became a part of our title.

Special thanks go to my business buddy, client, coach, and great friend, Veronika Palovska. You will never know how much your coaching has changed my life and transformed my business. Thank you for always saying "yes" to my crazy projects!

I thank my parents, who at one point sacrificed a lot of money so I could learn the language that I now call my "second." Nothing would have happened without that sacrifice.

Finally, my deepest gratitude goes to my family. My kids, Stephen and Vera, who taught me that spending all the day hours in front of the computer isn't the best time investment —

thank you for teaching me how to work smarter.

To Wimbai: thank you for believing in me when I was nothing but a knot of doubts. Your inspiration and encouragement made all the difference.

Veronika

First, I'd like to thank Elena for inviting me to join this adventure — and all the other adventures as well. It means everything to me.

My thanks go to my accomplices — people who have invested their time, energy, and money in my brand. You have made impossible things possible, and I'll never take you for granted. Special thanks to the pioneering members of my *#blog2teach* class and the ladies who have worked with me in the *Write with Clarity and Confidence* program.

Thanks to my grandpa for teaching me

everything I know about writing and about life, and to my grandma, who always believed in me. I hope you both are watching from up there.

Thanks to my mom, for *everything*.

Thanks to my teachers and mentors, especially Elena Mutonono (again), who helped me find my voice and find the courage to use it online, and Regina Anaejionu, who inspired me to choose this journey and taught me how to make a living teaching what I love and helping others do the same. Also, thank you both for making the online teaching industry so awesome.

About the authors

Elena Mutonono has been teaching online since 2008, trying out Skype lessons and buggy beta webinar software that few people in her home country of Ukraine knew how to use. In 2009, she received a grant from the Regional English Language Office at the US Embassy in Kyiv, Ukraine, to develop online training programs for school teachers.

After several years of teaching one-on-one, Elena began experimenting with different online business models that would allow online teachers to scale their businesses much faster while doing the things they loved and impacting more people with their messages of change.

Her focus now is smart online teaching that

helps teachers and coaches gain more creative and financial freedom.

Veronika Palovska transitioned online in 2016. Before that, she had run a private local language school for adults in her home country, the Czech Republic, while side-hustling online as a freelance graphic designer.

She started her blog, *Do You Speak Freedom*, to help non-native English-speaking entrepreneurs and freelancers work internationally without feeling handicapped. She soon shifted her focus, and now she works with online teachers and coaches from around the globe, no matter their native language.

She helps educators build websites and blogs that attract their dream clients so they can make a living teaching what they love and gain more freedom for themselves and the people they care about—their loved ones and their online community.

Further Resources

Ready to opt out of your *real job*?

Don't forget to download your *Opted Out Journal* (the digital version is free) with reflective questions and creative exercises to help you put the tips in practice: **optedoutlife.com/journal.**

Find more resources, personal help, and a free community at **optedoutlife.com.**

Endnotes

[i] Seth Godin, "define: Brand," December 13, 2009, http://sethgodin.typepad.com/seths_blog/2009/12/define-brand.html.

[ii] Alexandra Franzen, "Is it Possible to Run a Business Without Using Social Media?" August 20, 2015, http://www.alexandrafranzen.com/2015/08/20/is-it-possible-to-run-a-business-without-using-social-media.

[iii] Andrew Beattie, "Defining the 3 Types of Investment," last modified February 24, 2017, http://www.investopedia.com/articles/younginvestors/10/what-is-an-investment.asp.

[iviv] Breanne Dyck, "No one cares" blog post https://mnibconsulting.com/no-one-cares/

[v] Breanne Dyck, "How to Find your Ideal Customers Online" https://medium.com/@mnibreanne/in-a-recent-episode-of-10xtalk-erik-kerr-defined-marketing-as-two-things-5a467278328d

[vi] Breanne Dyck, *Beyond Satisfaction*. *http://beyondsatisfactionbook.com/*

www.ingramcontent.com/pod-product-compliance
Lightning Source LLC
Chambersburg PA
CBHW050107230526
45470CB00004B/1708